Educational and Series advisor Felicia Law

First published 1980 by
Octopus Books Limited
59 Grosvenor Street
London W1

© 1980 Octopus Books Limited

ISBN 0 7064 1363 6

Produced by Mandarin Publishers Limited
22a Westland Road, Quarry Bay, Hong Kong

Printed in Hong Kong

PDO 79-445

First Cook Book

by
Jennifer Fellows

illustrated by
Ann Rees

CONTENTS

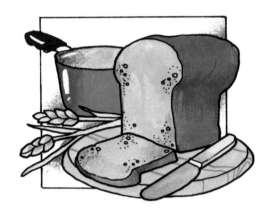
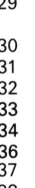

USING THE KITCHEN

Always wash your hands before you begin to cook.

A kitchen can be a dangerous place. Whenever you are going to use the cooker, always ask an adult to switch it on or light it for you.

Always turn pan handles inwards so you won't knock them over accidentally.

Never put your hands near the hot oven without oven gloves or mitts on.

Always read the recipe before you begin and make sure you have all the ingredients.

COOK'S EQUIPMENT

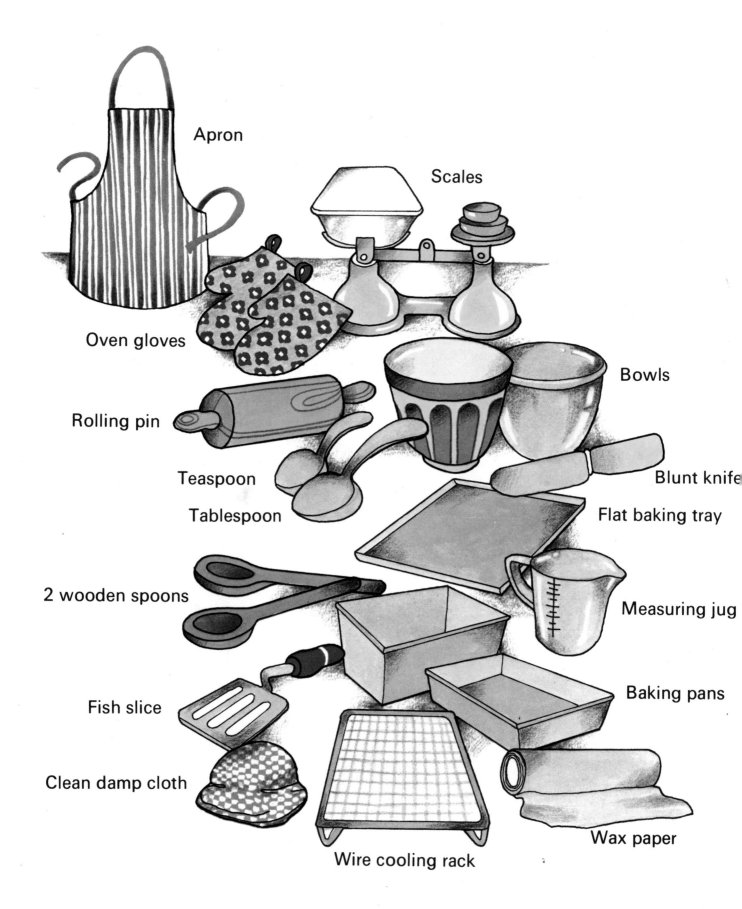

Apron

Scales

Oven gloves

Bowls

Rolling pin

Teaspoon

Blunt knife

Tablespoon

Flat baking tray

2 wooden spoons

Measuring jug

Fish slice

Baking pans

Clean damp cloth

Wax paper

Wire cooling rack

COOK'S LARDER

These basic ingredients will come into many of the recipes.

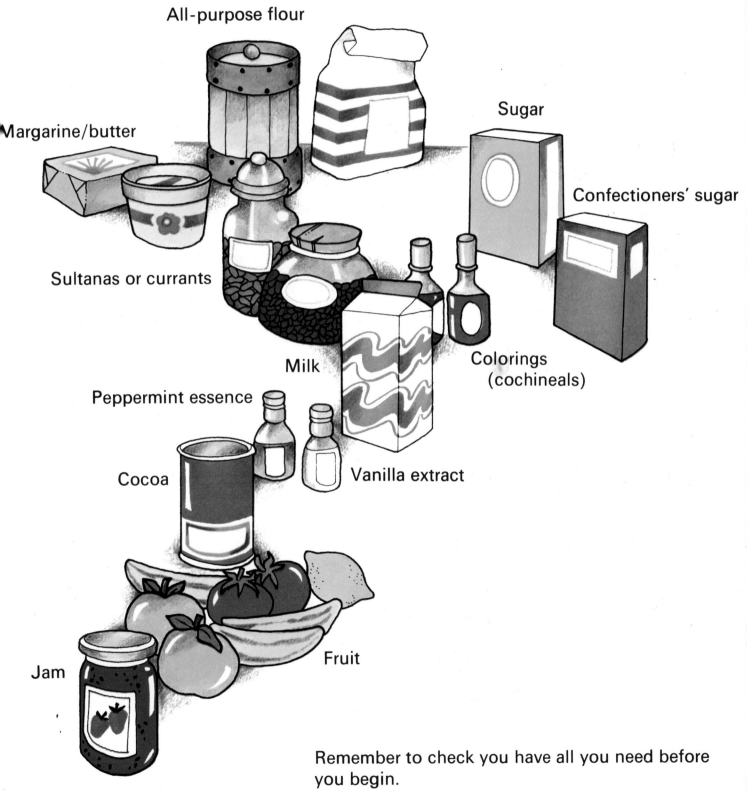

All-purpose flour

Sugar

Confectioners' sugar

Margarine/butter

Sultanas or currants

Milk

Colorings
(cochineals)

Peppermint essence

Cocoa

Vanilla extract

Jam

Fruit

Remember to check you have all you need before you begin.

COOK'S CODE

Always flour the table top before rolling out on it so that dough will not stick.

Always heat the oven before you begin so it can warm up.

How to knead: When kneading pastry, put it onto a floured top and press it with your fingers. Continue to fold it inwards and over, pressing it each time, about six times.

A pinch of salt is as much salt as you can hold between your thumb and first finger.

Always clean surfaces before and after you have used them.

When you mix sugar and butter/margarine, the mixture will turn pale yellow when it is fully blended.

Always grease and flour tins or trays before using them, to prevent the food from sticking.

COOKING WITHOUT A COOKER

In all these recipes, you are not going to use any heat. The different ingredients will mix together without being melted first.

Cheese and pineapple spike

Tin of pineapple slices or chunks
A piece of cheese
Cherries (glacé, tinned or fresh)
1 large potato
Tin foil, cocktail sticks,
knife, sieve, 2 plates

1 Wrap the potato in foil.

2 Carefully open the tin of pineapple. Using the sieve, pour off the juice.

3 4 Put the pineapple pieces onto a plate, and if they are not cubes, cut each slice into six or eight. On the other plate, cut the cheese into small pieces.

5 Skewer chunks of cheese and pineapple on a cocktail stick and wedge into potato.

6 Continue until the cheese and pineapple are finished.

7 Add a few cherries to give a more colorful effect.

12

Coconut ice shapes

1 small can of condensed milk
2¼ cups confectioners' sugar
¾ cup dessicated coconut
2 food colorings
Baking tray or plate, 2 bowls
sieve, wooden spoon, blunt knife

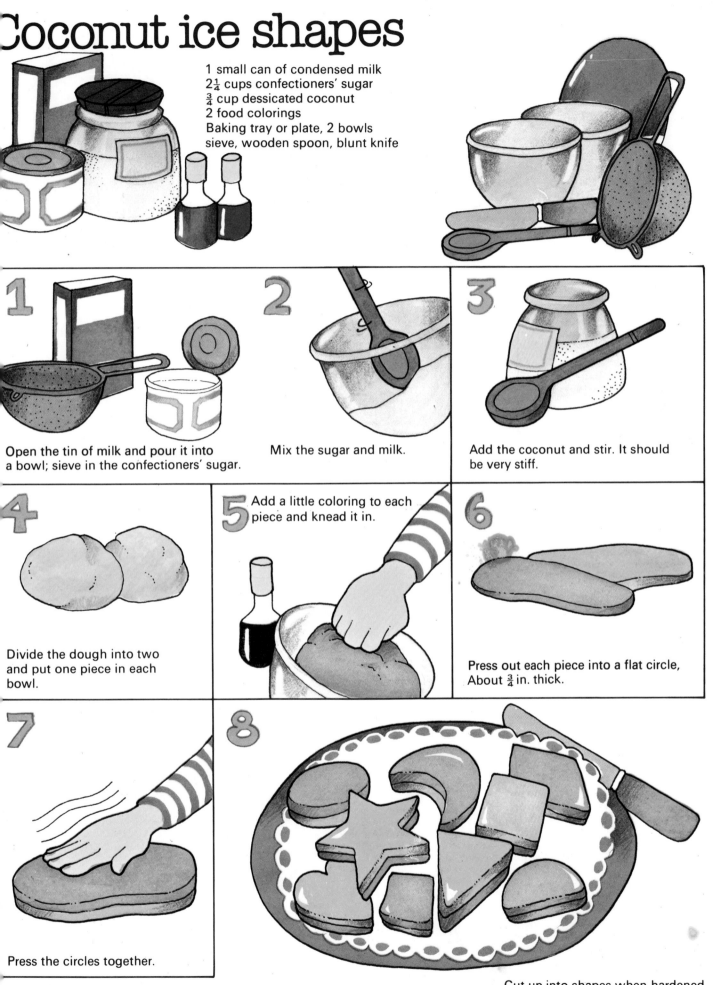

1 Open the tin of milk and pour it into a bowl; sieve in the confectioners' sugar.

2 Mix the sugar and milk.

3 Add the coconut and stir. It should be very stiff.

4 Divide the dough into two and put one piece in each bowl.

5 Add a little coloring to each piece and knead it in.

6 Press out each piece into a flat circle, About ¾ in. thick.

7 Press the circles together.

8 Cut up into shapes when hardened.

Salad sandwich boats

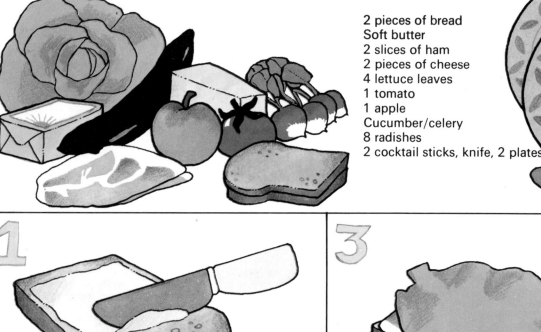

2 pieces of bread
Soft butter
2 slices of ham
2 pieces of cheese
4 lettuce leaves
1 tomato
1 apple
Cucumber/celery
8 radishes
2 cocktail sticks, knife, 2 plates

1

Butter the bread and put 1 slice on each plate.

2

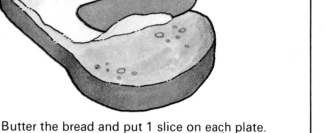

Place a piece of cheese in the middle of the sandwich boat and put apple and tomato pieces round it.

3

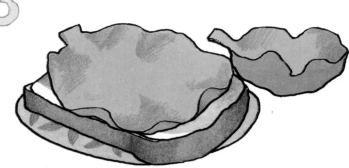

Decorate with a lettuce leaf and slice of ham.

4

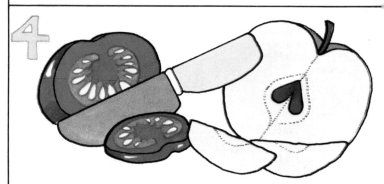

Cut the tomato into pieces and divide the apple into small slices.

6

Cut a piece of cucumber about 2½ in long and halve it. Divide each half into four long strips.

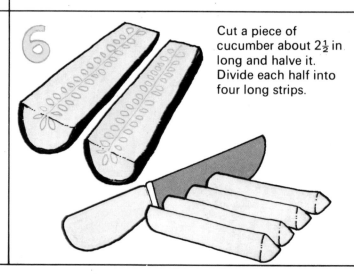

14

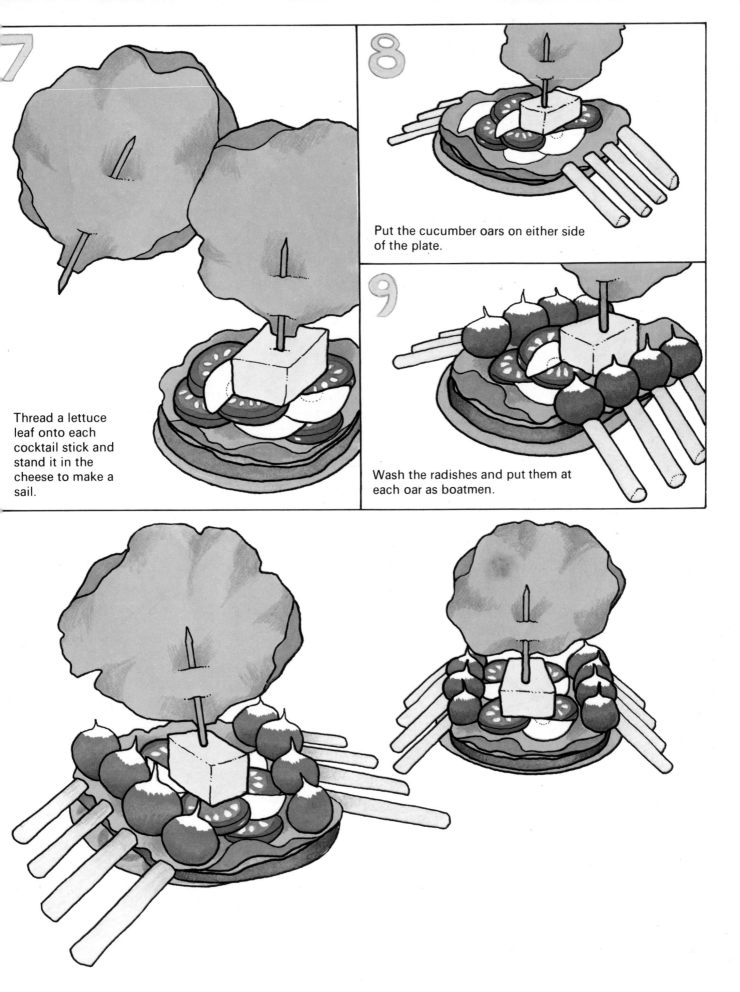

7

Thread a lettuce leaf onto each cocktail stick and stand it in the cheese to make a sail.

8

Put the cucumber oars on either side of the plate.

9

Wash the radishes and put them at each oar as boatmen.

Peppermint creams

3½ cups confectioners' sugar
1 egg white
½ lemon
Peppermint essence
Blunt knife, 2 bowls, cup and
saucer, sieve, wooden spoon,
rolling pin (or clean empty
bottle), 1 teaspoon

1 Sieve the confectioners' sugar into a bowl.

2 Divide the egg into white and yolk using a cup and saucer.

3 Put the egg white into the sugar and mix.

4 Knead well with your hands.

5 Add a little of the lemon juice and a few drops of peppermint essence. Knead again.

6 Pour a little sugar on the top of the table. Roll the mixture into a sausage.

7 Using a blunt knife, cut the sausage into small sweets.

8 Arrange the sweets on a plate and allow to harden.

Marzipan sweets

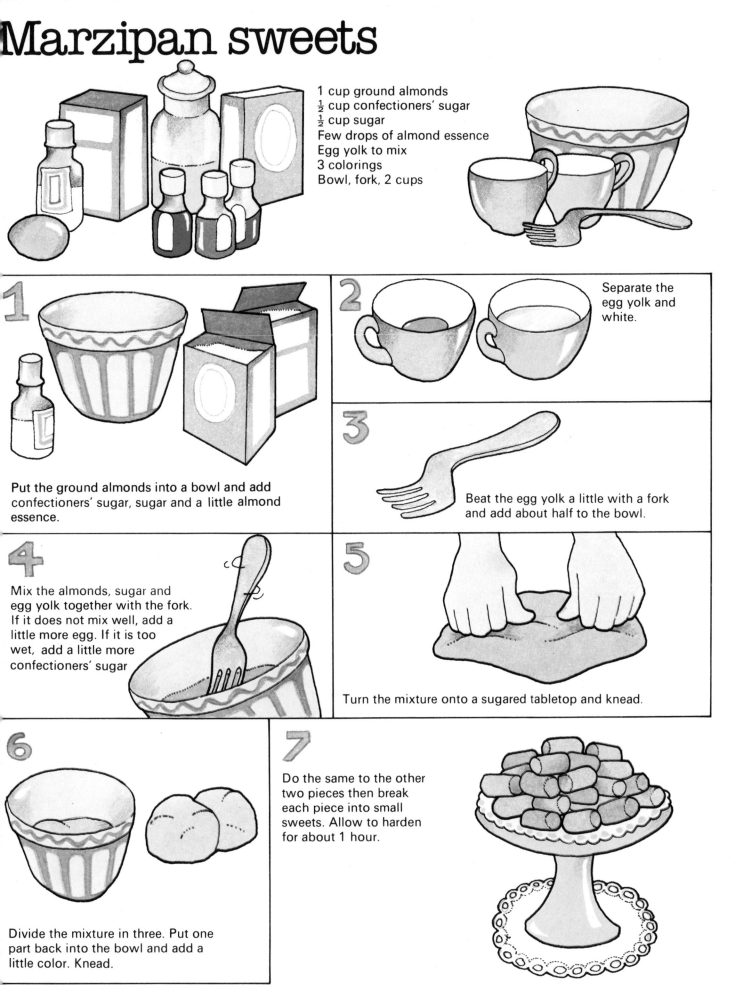

1 cup ground almonds
½ cup confectioners' sugar
½ cup sugar
Few drops of almond essence
Egg yolk to mix
3 colorings
Bowl, fork, 2 cups

1 Put the ground almonds into a bowl and add confectioners' sugar, sugar and a little almond essence.

2 Separate the egg yolk and white.

3 Beat the egg yolk a little with a fork and add about half to the bowl.

4 Mix the almonds, sugar and egg yolk together with the fork. If it does not mix well, add a little more egg. If it is too wet, add a little more confectioners' sugar

5 Turn the mixture onto a sugared tabletop and knead.

6 Divide the mixture in three. Put one part back into the bowl and add a little color. Knead.

7 Do the same to the other two pieces then break each piece into small sweets. Allow to harden for about 1 hour.

Milk shakes

2½ cups milk
Ice cream
Flavoring
4 glasses
1 jug
Whisk
Straws

1

If you don't have a blender:
Put 4 tablespoons of ice cream into a jug and pour on the milk. Add the flavoring and mix well.   Pour into glasses.

2

If you have a blender:
2½ cups milk, 4 tablespoons ice cream and any fruit you like (apple, banana, raspberry . . . . . .)
Wash the fruit and cut it into small pieces. Put the milk, ice cream and fruit into the blender. Blend and pour into glasses.

For a special occasion frost the glasses first:

piece of lemon
a glass
a saucer of sugar

Rub the lemon round the rim of the glass and then dip it into the sugar.

COOKING ON THE RINGS OR UNDER THE BROILER

Whenever you see this sign⬤ ask an adult to put the broiler or cooking ring on for you.

When you use the rings, the heat is rising through the ingredients. Stir the mixture constantly to spread the heat evenly.

Under the broiler, only the top of the food gets really hot.

In a skillet, you must turn the food over to cook on both sides.

Simple Croque Monsieur

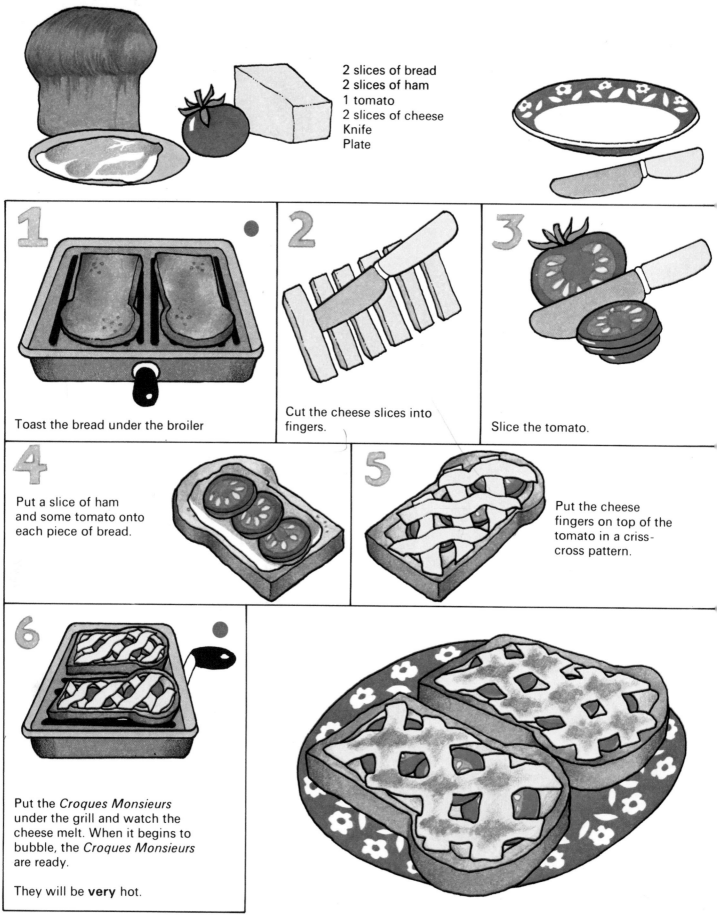

2 slices of bread
2 slices of ham
1 tomato
2 slices of cheese
Knife
Plate

1 Toast the bread under the broiler

2 Cut the cheese slices into fingers.

3 Slice the tomato.

4 Put a slice of ham and some tomato onto each piece of bread.

5 Put the cheese fingers on top of the tomato in a criss-cross pattern.

6 Put the *Croques Monsieurs* under the grill and watch the cheese melt. When it begins to bubble, the *Croques Monsieurs* are ready.

They will be **very** hot.

French toast

1 egg
pinch salt
2 tablespoons cold milk
2 slices of white bread
A little butter
Fork
Pudding bowl
Skillet
Fish slice

1 Break the egg into the bowl and whisk with the fork.

2 Add the milk and salt.

3 Dip each piece of bread thoroughly into the egg mixture.

4 Put the butter into the skillet over a medium flame or heat.

5 When the butter foams, put the bread into it and cook on each side.

6 Remove when both sides are browned.

You may have to cook one piece at a time unless you have a very large skillet

Scotch pancakes

2 cups all-purpose flour
$\frac{1}{4}$ teaspoon salt
1 egg
1 tablespoon sugar
$1\frac{1}{4}$ cups milk
A little shortening
Bowl
Wooden spoon
Large skillet
Cup
Large spoon
Fish slice
Fork

1

Put the flour and salt into the bowl and make a hollow in the middle.

2

Break the egg into the centre of the flour with a little milk. Begin to mix.

3

Go on adding the milk, a little at a time, stirring all the time.

4

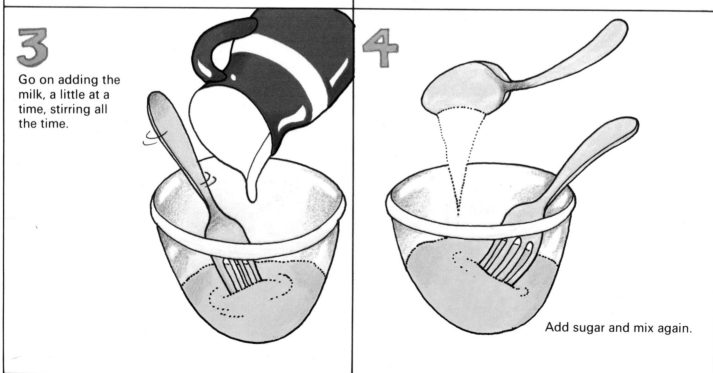

Add sugar and mix again.

5 Heat the skillet and put a little shortening so the pancake will not stick.

6 Put a spoonful of the mixture into the pan. When bubbles rise, turn it over to brown the other side.

7 Continue until all the mixture is used up.

Eat the pancakes cold with butter or hot sprinkled with caster sugar,

John's potato cakes

2½ cups cold mashed potato
1 cup flour
2½ tablespoons butter/margarine
Butter for afterwards
Bowl
Fork
Skillet
Fish slice

1 Put the cold mashed potato, flour and butter/margarine into the bowl and mix well with a fork.

2 Divide the mixture into about 12 little balls.

3 Flatten each ball until it is the size of a jam jar top and about ½ in thick.

Eat them whilst they are still hot with butter on top.

4 Fry the potato cakes in a dry skillet, turning once.

Cinnamon toast

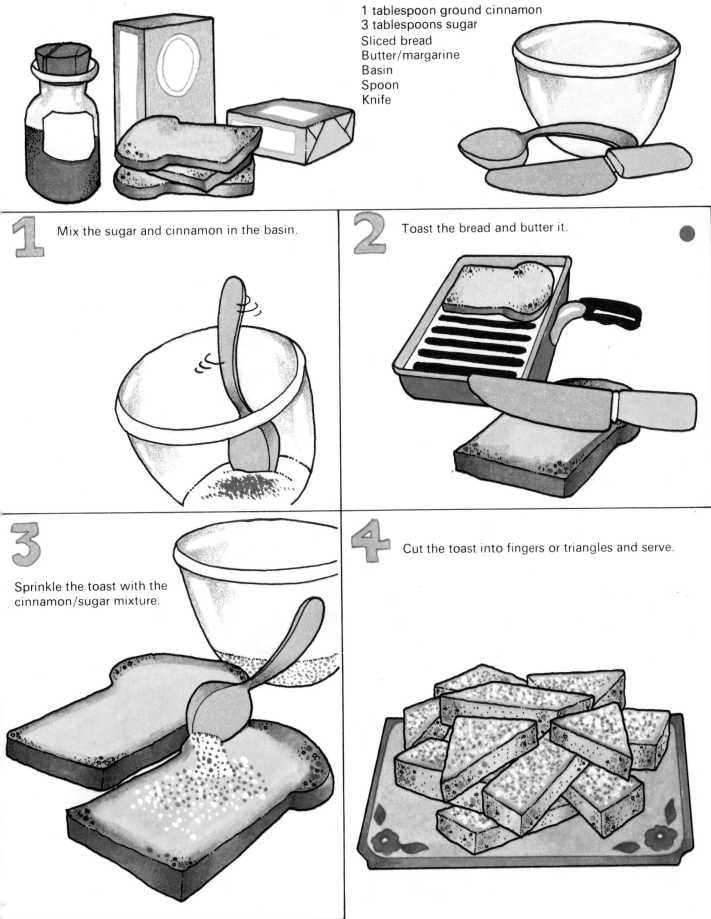

1 tablespoon ground cinnamon
3 tablespoons sugar
Sliced bread
Butter/margarine
Basin
Spoon
Knife

1 Mix the sugar and cinnamon in the basin.

2 Toast the bread and butter it.

3 Sprinkle the toast with the cinnamon/sugar mixture.

4 Cut the toast into fingers or triangles and serve.

French fingers

Can of sardines
Black pepper
Vinegar
Bread
Butter
Basin
Fork
Knife

1 Ask someone to open the can of sardines for you.

2 Put the sardines into the basin with a little black pepper and vinegar to taste, and mix with a fork.

3 Toast the bread and then butter it.

4 Spread the toast with the sardine mixture and cut into fingers.

Chocolate fudge pieces

⅓ cup plain chocolate
2 tablespoons margarine
1¼ cups confectioners' sugar
1 tablespoon of
   top of the milk
4 drop vanilla extract
Saucepan
Bowl
Small cake tin
Wooden spoon

1 Break up the chocolate into the saucepan and add the margarine.

2 Put the saucepan over a low heat until the chocolate melts, then stir in the milk and vanilla extract

3 Put the icing sugar into the bowl and pour on the chocolate mixture. Mix well.

4 Pour the mixture into the baking tin and leave it to cool.

5 When it is set, cut the fudge into little pieces.

Crispy chocolate cakes

¼ cup margarine
2 tablespoons margarine
1 tablespoon maple syrup
1 cup Breakfast Cereal
¼ cup unsweetened cocoa
¼ cup confectioners' sugar
Wooden spoon
Saucepan
Paper cake cases
Plate or tray
Spoon

1 Put the margarine and syrup into the saucepan and place on a low heat.

2 When they have melted remove the pan and mix the ingredients.

3 Add the sugar and the unsweetened cocoa and stir in well

4 Add the cereal and mix in very gently until they are covered in the chocolaty mixture.

5 Put the paper cake cases onto the tray (about 16 of them) and spoon the mixture into them (about 1 spoonful for each).

6 Leave them for about half-an-hour to cool.

COOKING IN THE OVEN

ood cooks in the oven, where it is surrounded by
eat. Heat rises, so the top of the oven is the warmest
art and the bottom the coolest.

lways wear oven gloves when taking things out of
he oven as they will be very hot.

emember, whenever you see ● ask an adult to switch
n or light the oven for you.

Shortcrust pastry

1⅔ cups all-purpose flour
½ cup margarine
2 tablespoons cold water
Mixing bowl
Knife
Sieve
Plate

1 Sieve the flour into a bowl.

2 Add the margarine in small pieces.

3 Using the tips of your fingers, rub the flour and margarine lightly together until it looks like breadcrumbs.

4 Add the water a little at a time until you have a thick dough.

5 If you have time, place your pastry dough in the refrigerator for 20 minutes before rolling out. This makes it stretchy and easier to use.

Jam tarts

Shortcrust pastry
Jam
Rolling pin
Teaspoon
Cup or pastry cutter
Tart tins.

1 Roll out the pastry on a floured tabletop, turning it round every now and then until $\frac{1}{4}$ in thick

2 With a cutter or cup, cut out your tarts. Press each one into a greased tart tin.

3 Put a teaspoon of jam into each tart. Do not overfill.

Regulo 4 or 350^F/180^C
Middle shelf
10 mins.

10mins.

Sausage rolls

Shortcrust pastry
6 chipolata sausages
Water
Knife
Baking tray

1 Make up shortcrust pastry as on previous page.

2 Cut the chipolatas into halves.

3 Roll out the pastry and cut it into four strips, each a little wider than the sausage halves.

4 Cut each strip widthways into two or three.

5 Roll a piece of sausage into each piece of pastry. Wet the edge of the pastry with your finger to help it stick.

6 Put the rolls onto the baking tray and cook.

Regulo 6
400°F/200°C
Middle shelf
20 mins.

20mins.

Cheese straws

1 cup all-purpose flour
¼ cup margarine
½ cup cheese
Pinch of salt
Pinch of pepper
Cold water
Teaspoon, grater
Bowl, baking sheet
Wire tray
Rolling pin
Dish, blunt knife

1 Grate the cheese onto a dish.

2 Put the flour and margarine into a bowl and mix with your fingers until it forms little crumbs.

3 Add the grated cheese, 4 teaspoons of water, and mix.

4 Continue to add water, a little at a time, until the dough sticks together but is not soggy.

5 Roll out the pastry on a floured tabletop until ½ in thick.

6 Cut it into fingers, or any shapes you like, and put them onto the greased baking tray to cook.

Regulo 4 or 350ᶠ/180ᶜ
Middle shelf
15 mins.

15mins.

7 Allow your cheese straws to cool on a wire tray.

Hot spicy muffins

2 cups all-purpose flour
½ teaspoon mixed spice
¼ cup shortening
2 tablespoons margarine
2 tablespoons sugar
½ cup sultanas
1 egg
1 apple
Teaspoon, grater
Bowl, cup
Baking tray, saucer
Rolling pin

1 Peel, core and grate the apple.

2 Put the flour and spice into the bowl, and rub in the shortening and margarine

3 Add the sugar and sultanas.

4 Mix to a soft dough with the egg and apple.

5 Sprinkle a little flour onto tabletop and roll out the dough, to about ½ in thickness.

6 Using the cup, cut out rounds and place them onto the greased baking tray.

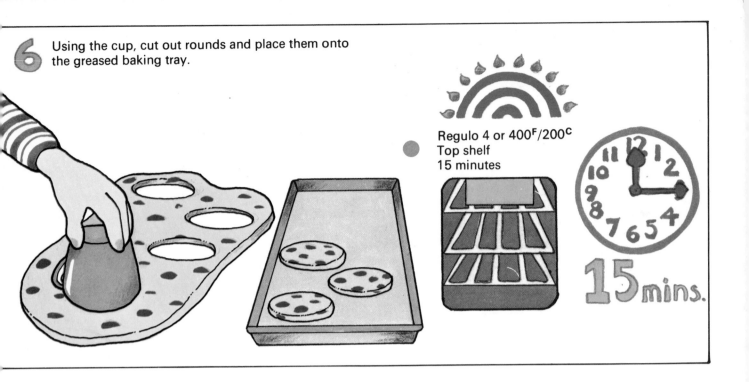

Regulo 4 or 400^F/200^C
Top shelf
15 minutes

15mins.

Iced buns

½ cup margarine
½ cup sugar
2 medium sized eggs
1 cup self-rising flour
⅔ cup confectioners' sugar
½ cup of water
Cochineal colorings
Bowl, wooden spoon
Paper cake cases
Baking tray

1 Mix margarine and sugar to a cream.

2 Add eggs one by one.

3 Add the self-rising flour and mix well.

4 Place paper cases on baking tray.

Half fill each case with mixture.

5 Regulo 5 or 375F/180C
Middle shelf
15 mins.

15 mins.

6 Mix confectioners' sugar and water, a little at a time, until thic

7 Divide icing into 3 cups and add different colours.

8 When cakes are cool decorate with icing.

Gingerbread snakes

¼ cup soft margarine
4 tablespoons sugar
1 tablespoon black treacle
1¼ cups all-purpose flour
1 tablespoon milk
1 tablespoon ground ginger
Bowl
Wooden spoon
Baking tray

1 Mix margarine and sugar.

2 Add the black treacle, and mix.

3 Add the all-purpose flour ginger and milk and mix well.

4 On a floured table top, shape the mixture into small balls.

5 Shape the balls into lengths then into snakes.

6 Place the snakes on a greased baking tray and cook.

7 Regulo 4 or 350^F/180^C
Top shelf
15 mins.

15 mins.

Apple puffs

2 cooking apples
  or a tin of apple sauce
6 teaspoons sugar
a little flour
1 packet defrosted
  puff pastry
Rolling pin
Baking tray
Cup of water
Blunt knife
Plate
Fish slice

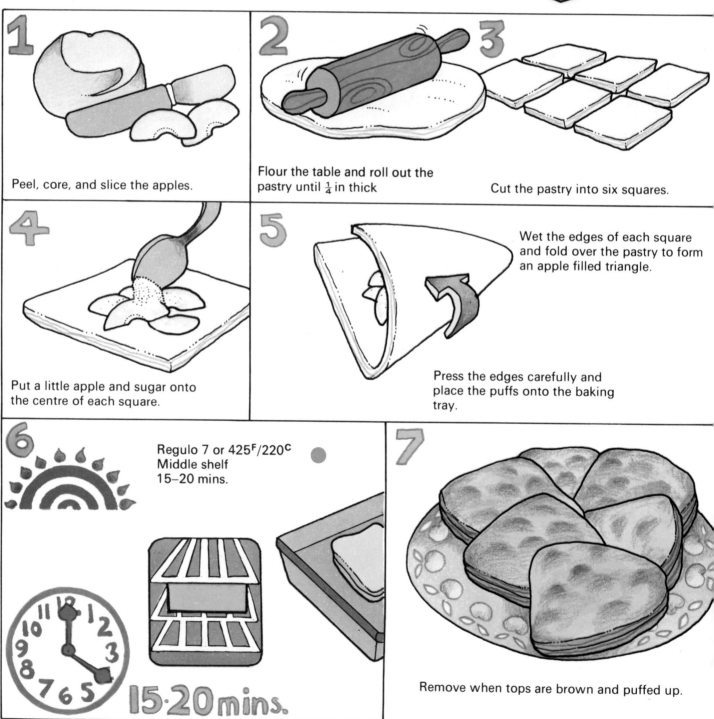

1 Peel, core, and slice the apples.

2 Flour the table and roll out the pastry until $\frac{1}{4}$ in thick

3 Cut the pastry into six squares.

4 Put a little apple and sugar onto the centre of each square.

5 Wet the edges of each square and fold over the pastry to form an apple filled triangle.

Press the edges carefully and place the puffs onto the baking tray.

6 Regulo 7 or 425^F/220^C
Middle shelf
15–20 mins.

15·20 mins.

7 Remove when tops are brown and puffed up.

Chocolate button buns

¼ cup margarine or butter
4 tablespoons sugar
1 egg
Vanilla extract
¾ cup all-purpose flour
½ cup chocolate buttons
Bowl, wooden spoon
Cup, tablespoon
Baking tray
Teaspoon
Cooling tray
Fish slice

1 Put the margarine/butter and sugar into a bowl and mix well.

2 Break the egg into a cup, add a few drops of vanilla essence, and mix.

3 Put the egg mixture into the bowl and mix well.

4 Add the flour and stir in with a tablespoon.

5 Break up the chocolate buttons and add them to the mixture.

6 Using the teaspoon, drop the mixture onto a greased baking tray to form small round cakes.

Regulo 4 or 350ᶠ/180ᶜ
Middle shelf
10 mins.

10mins.

7 Allow to cool on wire tray.

Banana bread

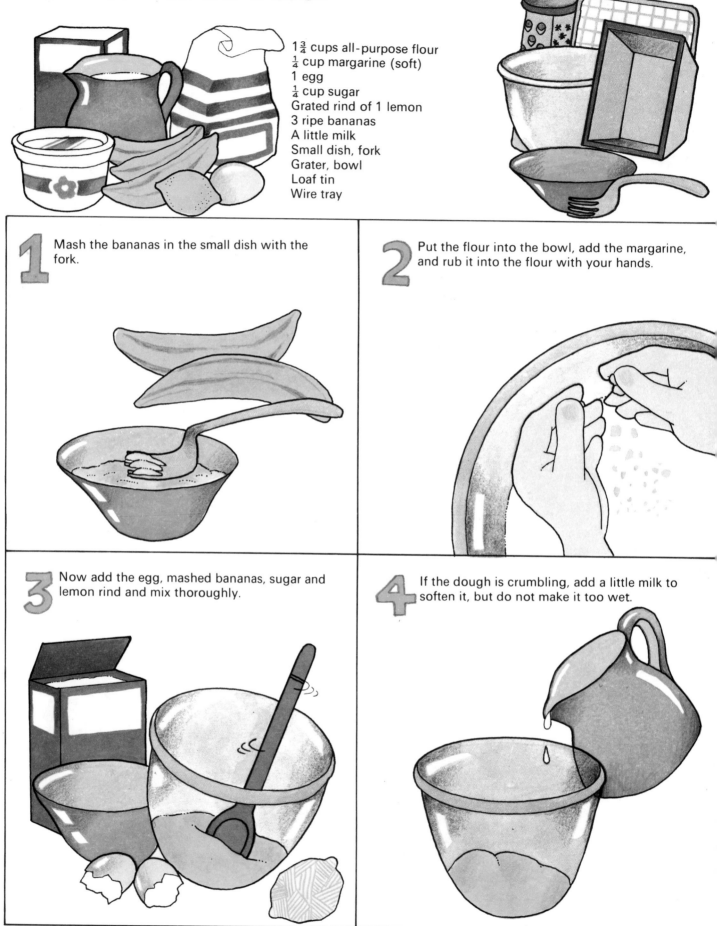

1¾ cups all-purpose flour
¼ cup margarine (soft)
1 egg
¼ cup sugar
Grated rind of 1 lemon
3 ripe bananas
A little milk
Small dish, fork
Grater, bowl
Loaf tin
Wire tray

1 Mash the bananas in the small dish with the fork.

2 Put the flour into the bowl, add the margarine, and rub it into the flour with your hands.

3 Now add the egg, mashed bananas, sugar and lemon rind and mix thoroughly.

4 If the dough is crumbling, add a little milk to soften it, but do not make it too wet.

5

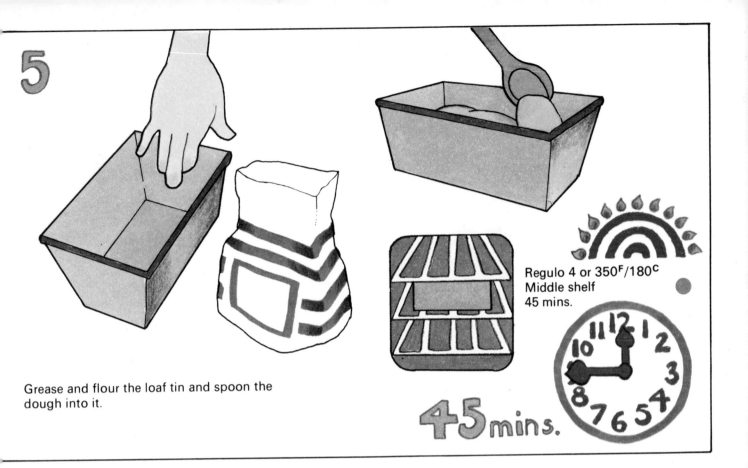

Regulo 4 or 350^F/180^C
Middle shelf
45 mins.

45mins.

Grease and flour the loaf tin and spoon the dough into it.

6

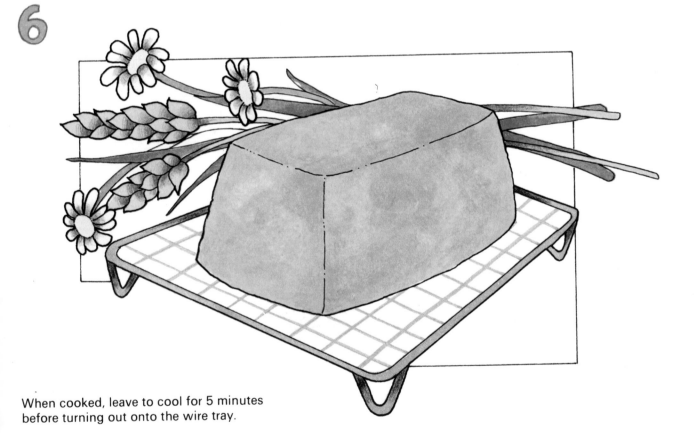

When cooked, leave to cool for 5 minutes before turning out onto the wire tray.

Brownies

1 cup all-purpose flour
¼ teaspoon bicarbonate
    of soda
Pinch salt
¼ cup shortening
½ cup sugar
2 tablespoons water
1 packet chocolate chips or
    buttons (about ⅔ cup)
2 eggs
¼ cup chopped walnuts
Greaseproof paper
Baking tin
Saucepan
Wooden spoon

1 Put the shortening, sugar and water into a saucepan. Stir them over a moderate heat until melted.

2 Take the saucepan off the stove and mix in the chocolate chips until melted also.

3 Add the eggs, one at a time, and mix well.

4 Add the flour, bicarbonate of soda and salt, and heat.

5 Lastly, add the chopped walnuts.

6

Line the tin with greased greaseproof paper.

7 Pour in the mixture and cook.

Regulo 4 or 350^F/180^C
Middle shelf
25 mins.

25mins.

8 When the Brownie mixture is cooked, leave it to cool and then cut into about twelve pieces.

Currant biscuits

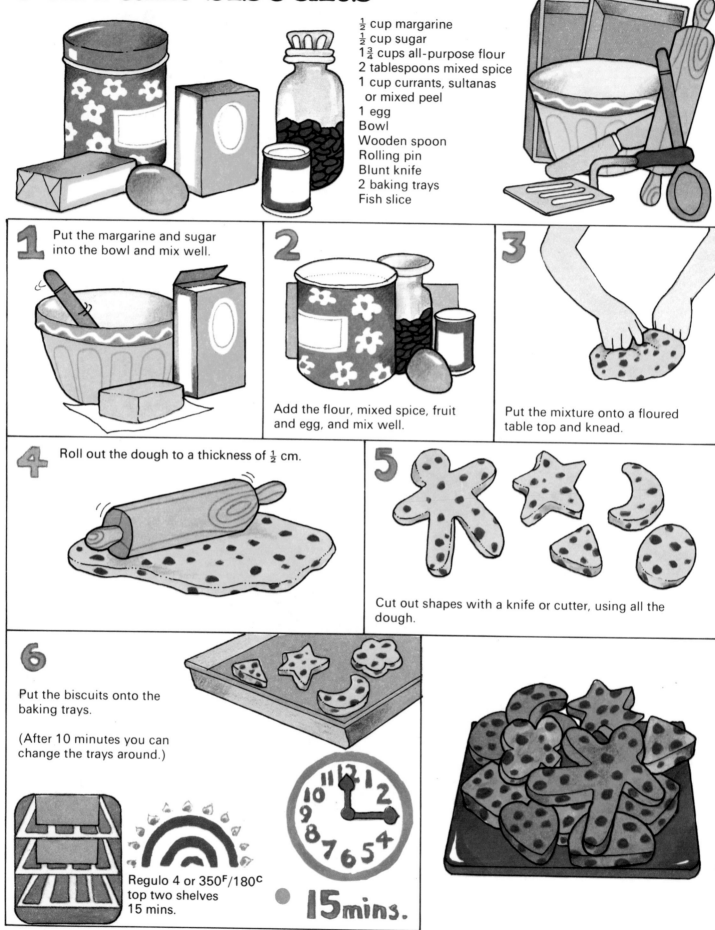

½ cup margarine
½ cup sugar
1¾ cups all-purpose flour
2 tablespoons mixed spice
1 cup currants, sultanas
  or mixed peel
1 egg
Bowl
Wooden spoon
Rolling pin
Blunt knife
2 baking trays
Fish slice

1 Put the margarine and sugar into the bowl and mix well.

2 Add the flour, mixed spice, fruit and egg, and mix well.

3 Put the mixture onto a floured table top and knead.

4 Roll out the dough to a thickness of ½ cm.

5 Cut out shapes with a knife or cutter, using all the dough.

6 Put the biscuits onto the baking trays.

(After 10 minutes you can change the trays around.)

Regulo 4 or 350ᶠ/180ᶜ
top two shelves
15 mins.

15mins.

Shortbread

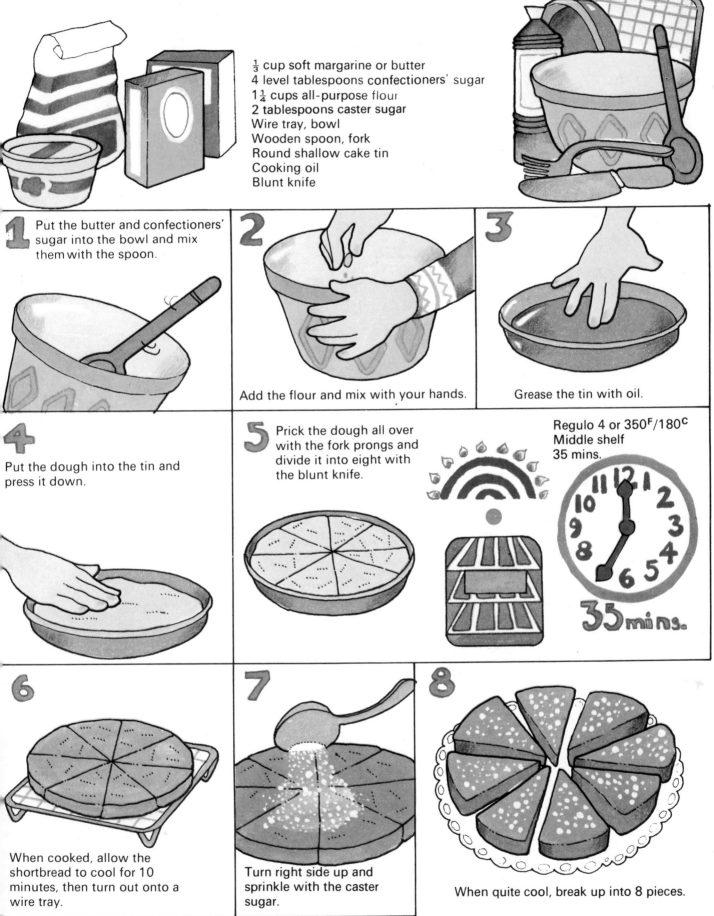

⅓ cup soft margarine or butter
4 level tablespoons confectioners' sugar
1¼ cups all-purpose flour
2 tablespoons caster sugar
Wire tray, bowl
Wooden spoon, fork
Round shallow cake tin
Cooking oil
Blunt knife

1 Put the butter and confectioners' sugar into the bowl and mix them with the spoon.

2 Add the flour and mix with your hands.

3 Grease the tin with oil.

4 Put the dough into the tin and press it down.

5 Prick the dough all over with the fork prongs and divide it into eight with the blunt knife.

Regulo 4 or 350°F/180°C
Middle shelf
35 mins.

35 mins.

6 When cooked, allow the shortbread to cool for 10 minutes, then turn out onto a wire tray.

7 Turn right side up and sprinkle with the caster sugar.

8 When quite cool, break up into 8 pieces.

45